जोवियल जेम

AKASH

वड़र्स ऑफ सोल फैमिली

यह किताब हम सबके प्यारे CEO और भाई आकाश चौरसिया जी के जन्मदिवस के उपलक्ष्य में वइर्स ऑफ़ सोल परिवार द्वारा आयोजित अन्थोलोजी के माध्यम से उन्हें एक प्यारा सा उपहार दिया गया है । जहां सारे लेखक , लेखिकओं कोरे पन्नों पर अपने भाई के प्रति भावनाओं को व्यक्त किया हैं जिनके आयोजक वइर्स ऑफ़ सोल प्रकाशन द्वारा किया गया है

क्रम-सूची

क्रम-सूची

About Publication

Words of Soul is a writing Community, where we have a group of new budding writers with their talent of framing emotions into words.

Formed by Dr. Nikita Dudagi and Lucky Pandey on May 15th 2021 to encourage and appreciate the enthusiastic writers. Weekly Special events and programs are being conducted to recognise the best Writer of the community. Words of Soul, a Group of Aspiring writers who ink the emotions of their heart to inspire the reader's mind.

Words of Soul Publications is not only a publication, it's a kind of family of writers which includes Co-author, writer, Author, compiler, co- compiler, Graphic Team, Project

Heads, CEO, co-founder and Founder.

Here Everyone is free to give their ideas and we initiate their actions.

Words of Soul Publications is growing day by day because of their friendly behaviour and Good Leadership for the team and writers.

1. Silky Jain

सिल्की जैन कोटा (राजस्थान) से है । उन्होंने अपनी पढ़ाई कोटा से ही पूरी की है । व्यवसाय प्रबंधन में स्नातकोत्तर करने के साथ ही उन्होंने कम्पनी सेक्रेटरी (Company Secretary) भी किया है । वह एक कम्पनी सेक्रेटरी है और उन्हें लिखना बहुत पसंद है । वे कई तरह - तरह की प्रतियोगिताओं में भाग ले चुकी है । लिखना, पढ़ना, गाना, पढ़ाना, घूमना, नई - नई चीज़ें करना और सीखना उनकी रूचियाँ है ।

प्यारा सा एहसास - मेरा आकाश

बारिश की पहली फुहार सा है वो।

दूर होकर भी पास सा है वो ।

जिससे बस बात करने से ही, मिल जाए खुशी ।

कुछ ऐसे अनोखे एहसास सा है वो ।

पहेली नहीं है कोई, पर फिर भी राज़दार सा है वो ।

बयां ना हो सके जो लफ़्ज़ों में, कुछ ऐसे अनकहे अल्फ़ाज़ सा है वो ।

जिससे अगर कोई एक बार मिल ले, तो उसे भूले ना कभी ।

कुछ ऐसा, खुशमिजाज़ सा है वो।

सबके दिलों की धड़कन बहुत ख़ास सा है वो ।

मेरे चेहरे का नूर, एक पूरी हुई अरदास सा है वो ।

2. Sudhanya Nath

Dr. Sudhanya Nath is a veterinarian (Animal Nutritionist) from Odisha, India. She is currently pursuing her PhD degree from WBUAFS, Kolkata, West Bengal, India. She was conferred Inkzoid Book of World Records 2021, GO Inkzodiac Award 2021, OMG Book of Records 2021, Glorious Book of World Records 2021, InSc Young Achiever Award 2020, Vajra World Records 2020, International Research Awards 2020 on New Science Inventions, Inspiring Lady Veterinarian Award 2021, Fame Fever Award 2021, Aminorich Netherlands Award 2022 etc. She has contributed in more than 100 anthologies. She is Founder of World of Logophiles (WOL), Disciple Head of Inked Solace Community (ISC), Community Head of Inner Souls (IS) and Author Revolution (AR). On 4th October 2020, she was recognized by Times of India and local newspaper Dharitri of Odisha for making the best use of lockdown by achieving 325 e-certificates through various webinars, quiz and competitions.

AKASH CHAURASIYA

A - A sweet boy with lots of dream in his eyes,

K - Kind, well-mannered guy who is the most active (sarcastically) being a core member,

A - Achieving heights with zeal and dedication have been always his aim,

S - Surrounding himself with positive vibes, he shines all the time,

H - Hope he always keep smiling and prospering.

C - Collabing with any write-up is his forte,

H- He always follows his heart and spread joy,

A - Aids all at the time of need,

U - Unique in his meme adroitness,

R - Radiance can be observed in his amazing writing skills,

A - A chap who has the ability to conquer everything what his heart desires,

S - Sober and down to Earth soul,

I - Inspiring all is his genre,

Y - Yielder of many great things,

A - A very happy B'Day Dear AKASH !!

3. Antra Choudhary

अंतरा चौधरी, नागपुर महाराष्ट्र की निवासी हैं । वह पिछले कुछ सालों से लिख रही हैं। उन्हें लिखने का शौक हैं ।उन्हें भ्रमण करना भी बहुत पसंद है । वह कहती हैं की जज़्बातों को लिखकर ज़ाहिर करने से दिल को सुकून मिलता हैं और लिखकर दिल की बात ज़ाहिर करना भी एक कला हैं। उन्हें पढ़ना और लिखना दोनों पसंद हैं ।

वो खुद को खुशनसीब मानती हैं की वह बहुत ही सरल भाषा में लिखती हैं ताकि सब पढ़ सकें।

संपर्क करने हेतु -

इंस्टाग्राम - antarachoudhury.15

आकाश : प्यारा सा भाई

छोटी - छोटी खुशियों में खुश हो जाता है,

प्यारी प्यारी बातों से सबको हंसाया करता है,

कभी मैं बुलाऊं अगर कोई काम से

सबसे पहले मेरी बात सुनकर

पूरा वो करता है ,

जब मुझे किसी के बातों से गुस्सा आ जाता है,

अपनी अतरंगी हरकतों से

मेरे गुस्से को पिघलाया करता है,

हर एक काम वो वक़्त पर करता है,

मेरा भाई आकाश सबके काम अकेले ही कर लेता है,

उसके काम के इतनी तारीफ़ करते है

कि अपने भी काम मेरे भाई से करवाते है,

आकाश प्यारा सा भाई है मेरा

किसी को ना बोलकर किसी का दिल दुखाया नहीं करता

यही खूबी है जिसकी वजह से सबको प्यारा लगे ।।

4. Apeksha Khedekar

Apeksha Khedkar , a Young Writer. She Is 14 years girl ,from Pune. She is a Co-author And Compiler. She started writing from past 2 years . She writes Poems ,Shayari, Stories And Articles in 3 language English ,Marathi and Hindi on love ,life ,nature beauty ,success and many more! It feels her connected to herself as she explore herself every moment. Inking her emotions and feelings is the best company of her life . Writing is her passion . And She is Also A Great Dancer. Her aim is to achieve success in short time! To contact

her Instagram I'd - @words.of.apeksha
Email - apekshak225@gmail.comApeksha

Akash Bhaiyaa

Happy Janamdin

Bas sone ki baat krta hai tu pura din

Mera jina mushkil hota hai tere bin

Teri cuteness pe fida hu main

Sabse alag aur lajwab tu hain

Sabke maan main jaga kar leta hain tu

Par ek baat puchu

Sabse teri khushiyan btataa hai tu

Pr kabhi ghum nahi batata hai tu kyu ?

Hai to badaa kanjus tu

Pehle sir aur aaj pagal ye journey boht hi beautiful hai

Hamesha mere aise hi sath rehnaa

Aur meri bhabhi ko bhi jaldi lana phirse ek baar

Happy walaa Janamdin mere pyaare cute Bhaiyaa

Love you so muchh .

5. Marisha Dhar

Hailing from West Bengal ,Marisha Dhar is an ardent author who inks down poetry ,a source of inspiration for most readers .She is the HOD of Hindi PoetryDept in WOS Publication and with the honour of a Content Writer and School Campus Captain from Bharat Girl Up, she works to inspire the youth of India to inspire women to dow. Currently in X, she is pursuing her education from the Future Foundation School and with the believe in a better tomorrow she carries to stage her roles as an Author, Compiler and Co - Author !

Diamonds Sparkle

The stars glimmer,

In its own rhyme.

The river gushes ,

In our dream hive.

Nature beautifies,

Our bond strengthens.

Flowers paint the canvas,

Starry moments richen.

A fine day suddenly knocks,

With glitters festooning the way.

A new errand is about to begin,

As the candles are blown away.

You are the thousand stars,

That constitute my sky.

Luminates light when I fall,

To raise me pretty high.

Diamonds sparkle and vanish,

Tracing our souls' love.

We stand far apart,

Embracing our art !

6. Rahul B R

He is Rahul.B.R

He was born in 19/09/1999 Ramanagara district,
Karnataka.

But he is perceiving his higher studies in Bangalore.
He has completed bachelor degree in science. He like
to know more about literature and want to study more
and more about it...

He started writing poems from past four years and he
writes all kinds of poems... on life, about nature's
beauty, love and much more. He is coauthored in
many books, Compiler of the book called "The Song
Of Nature", "Nemophilist", "An Unchosen Bond" and

"Wings To Your Thoughts" and also his poems has been published in his college magazine too.

Letter To My Brother

Akash Chaurasiya

My dear brother,

Thanks for being my well-wisher.

You are my incomparable,

Joyful and loving label.

Like you there is no one,

You are the only one.

Always be smiling,

With purity and loving.

Your support is the best,

In the situation of worst.

Thanks for being with us,

To have you it's like bless.

7. Urmi Joshi

Her name is Urmi Joshi. She lives in shihor small
village located in Gujarat.
She is student of Bachelor of education and wanted to
be teacher one day. She did her Graduation in art's
stream with English literature as her main subject. She

started her writing journey one year ago. As now she is Co Author of 150 plus books and vajara world record holder as well. She loves to write in her regional language Gujrati apart from that she writes in Hindi and English as well. She just started her writing journey and want to reach high goals in her writing career.

नाम उसका आकाश

नाम उसका आकाश हैं पर मेरा हैं वो अक्षू ब्रो

हर मायने में वो दुकान हैं

चाहे वो लिखना हों पॉडकास्ट बनाना हों

या इमोजिस भेजना हों

पर दिल का बहुत अच्छा हैं

मदद सबकी करता हैं

प्यार से बातें सबसे करता हैं

पर हां !! अपने आप को कम हैंडसम समझता हैं

तस्वीरों की दुकान हैं

फिर इसकी उसकी वीडियो बनाके दो दीदी खाता मेरी जान हैं

मेरी लेखन क्षेत्र के सफ़र का श्रेय उसिको जाता हैं

दूर होके भी साथ निभाना उसीको आता हैं।

बस एक लड़की मिल जाएं

बस एक लड़की मिल जाएं ताकी वैले मीमीस बनाना छोड़ दे

इस वाले जन्मदिन पर उन्नति, प्रगति, सफ़लता, सवस्थता, आयुषयता,
यें सारी.... सब मेरे अक्षु ब्रो को मिल जाएं।

8. Lucky Pandey

Name:-Lucky Pandey
DOB:- 10-4-2004
Place:- Lawhar(Ballia) (Uttarpradesh)
Lucky pandey is a multiple record holder,
He is the author of solo book "Ankhir Kyu" which
contains poetry on the theme as "rape" which contains
bilingual too & is enough to teach the lesson of
humanity and also author of book "Pyar ka Ehsas"

Which is the collection of poetry on the theme of love in trilangual language.

His Ankhir kyu book is recorded in the (Indian Book of Record) Inkzoid book of world Record & "His Pyar ka Ehsas" book also recognized by "Inkzoid book of world record" (Glorious book of world record) Go Inkzoid award and by most precious award The "Backpenning award"

He is featured by fox interviewer U.S news portal and in Daily hunt news and in many more.

He is the Co-founder of writing community (words of soul) which has 200+ writers which continuously working hard and "wos" hosting lots of event such as jugalbandi, Insta contest, youtube contest daily challenge etc.

He is the compiler of Book "Ill concern" & Aurat teri yahi khani and co-author in many anthology.

Story of our CEO

This is the beautiful story of a gentleman and this story start with the planning of Dr.Nikita Dudagi and Lucky Pandey both started planning to open their own community after lot's of planning and strategy both decided to open their community on 15 of May 2021 named "Words Of Soul" (WOS) and after opening writing community. They were totally clueless about it that this is going to be very difficult task for them to arrange staff and all for community.

But this difficulty was chase by them in a easy way because of friendly and joyful nature of Dr.Nikita Dudagi & Lucky Pandey.

At that time Dr.Nikita brought her friend Pooja Desai as graphic designer(Ex-graphic designer of WOS) she worked so hard and was working so dedicatedly that she had become backbone of the community and than community start growing rapidly in the leadership of Dr.Nikita Dudagi. Everything was going so good we were happy by our team work. But wait this was not the end, suddenly graphic designer gave us a shocking surprise by announcing her resignation from her post at that time the pressure got doubled on Dr.Nikita Dudagi and Lucky Pandey both worked 24×7 and after few days came the gentleman and X-factor of WOS community or you can say blessing of WOS and the name of that person was "Akash Chaurasiya"

C.E.O of WOS publication.

He joined WOS as a community head and started making his place in the hearts of Dr.Nikita and in other writers too...

Days past, than Dr.Nikita trusted Akash more and more by seeing his hard work but, Lucky Pandey wanted to check the work of Akash because Lucky din't want to take risk anymore because they severed a lot in the past so he was thinking about future struggles if this same thing happened again than they both had to face trouble again, so because that the situations of community was under control but this man Akash Chaurisya continuously worked hard for WOS and this lead him to become the C.E.O of the WOS publication dated on 1st jan 2022.

Dr.Nikita and Lucky Pandey appointed Akash Chaurisya as a C.E.O of the WOS publications because of his dedication and the way of his execution of planning that was given by him.

This help WOS community to become Trusted, friendly and well mannered publication. Without the support of Akash Chaurisya and Antara Choudhury(Graphic head) it was too much difficult to make WOS as publication.

At the present time we have More than 200+ writers in our group and this will be uncountable after few years. We would like to say thanks to all my core members, participants, graphic designers and C.E.O Akash Chaurisya for joining our WOS family and making it more amazingly charming and today is that gentleman's birthday so I wish him many more returns of the day. May this hard work brings lots and lots of new ideas and happiness to his life. Really we are so lucky to have you and we are blessed to work with a man like you, glad to have you in our WOS family, once again a very happy birthday…

9. Poonam Shrivastava

पूनम श्रीवास्तव स्नातकोत्तर (मनोविज्ञान) बी एड हैं । ये सामाजिक पहलुओं के प्रति अपने मनोभावों को अपने लेखन के माध्यम से समाज तक पहुंचाने का पूरा प्रयास करती हैं ।पहले भी वह सह लेखिका के रूप में कई एंथोलॉजी का हिस्सा रही हैं उनका अपना पेज है "भावपूर्णम" जिस पर उनकी रचनाएं संकलित होती है ।

अक्षू का जन्मदिन

अक्षु हमसबका प्यारा, लाडला दुलारा है ,

इंक योर वर्ड्स का ,चमकता हुआ सितारा है!

है सबसे छोटा पर,सबसे अलग और न्यारा है,

हम बिठाते इसे अपने, पलको पर ,

ये हम सबके आंख का ,तारा है !!

आशीष देती मैं सदा ,शुभकामना है ये मेरी

दुख न आए राह में, खुशियां हों झोली में तेरी!

उन्नत शिखर पर चढ़ जाओ, इंसान आदर्श बन जाओ,

काट बाधाओं को सारे, बढ़ते कदम न ठहराओ!!

एक दिन ऐसा आएगा, अपना जहां बसाओगे,

काम तुम ऐसा करोगे, नाम जग में कमाओगे!

ऊंचे तुम उठ जाओगे जब , धरती पे ही पांव टिकाओगे

कहती है पूनम तुमसे ये, दिल में सबके बस जाओगे!!

मुबारक हो जन्मदिन तुमको, देती दिल से बधाई हूं!

फूलो फलों आगे बढ़ो ,करती ईश्वर से दुहाई हूं!!

10. Ritu

She is Ritu. She hailing from delhi.Her Passion is a writing and hobbies is reading and travelling... Her aim is to achieve success in a short time.

She want to become a professional writer in his life she completed 50+ anthology books as a co author contact with her through Gmail rituk5178@gmail.com /

Best friend

Friends grow up together,

Having endless conversations

About everything and nothing.

They confide in each other,

Telling only one another their

Innermost thoughts and secrets.

They have a friendship like no other,

A friendship bond that can't be broken.

We have all of this and more,

And for that, I am forever grateful.

Some friends will always come and go,

But you have always been there for me,

Never further than a phone call away.

To me, you will always be a true

Best friend

Have the most incredible birthday,

My dear. Continue living life to the

Full, filling it with as many joyous

Moments as you can.

Happy birthday akashuu sir♥?

11. Jaswalini Baral

She is Jaswalini Baral.She usually hails from Bhubaneswar, Odisha. She is a btech graduate. She used to keep different kinds of skills within herself as she feels that a person can acquires any kind of skills if he/she desires to. She has written for about 200 anthologies. She used to write poems on realistic things. Her main focus is to be government employee and a successful writer. To contact her . Instagram I'd

- @iam__jas__

WO JO HAR KISIKO HASAYE

Naam uska akshay hai,

Sab ko hasana uska lakshya hai..

Pyaar se usko hum bulate hai akshu,

Wo kehta hai mein ap sabke pyaar ke bina adhura rahu..

Bade hi majedaar hai ye ladka,

Hasa de apne memes se usko jisko laga ho sadka..

Bade hi shaandar kavita rachna karta hai,

Sacchi zubaani de kar be-jaan si kavitayon mein sach
much ka jaan bhar deta hai..

Jab dekho ye sabko hasane lage,

Chahe jo bhi ho ye sab ko apna hi maane..

Lakh duaayein hum sab bas uske liye maangte rahe,

Zindagi ki is rail gaadi mein ye bas aage badhta hi rahe..

Dil jesa iska sachha aur immandar hai,

Wese hi iska har ek kaam chamakdaar hai..

Dosto ka dost hai ye,

Chote chote bhai beheno ke bhai ye..

Kisiko apna pyaar batne mein koi kasar nehi chodta,

Bade hi husiyaar ye ladka hai apne maje mein hi rehta..

12. Durlav Sarkar

Durlav Sarkar is the founder of INKZOID FOUNDATION(the best publishing start-up and the fastest growing entrepreneurship) *which helped people to publish book for free during covid situation* ,who is a celebrity entrepreneur,multiple world record holder (only triple hat-trick world record holder) and the youngest world record strategist of Asia being the youngest speaker at Safalta Talks and many other talkshow.

He is also a poet, motivational speaker, influencer and works as a social activist as well famous for his 55 lyrical sonnets and each one of it was written within 5 mins.Six books were written on him as a tribute to him for all of his works and he was also awarded 'Best Start-up 2021' in support of West Bengal Government for his entrepreneurship being the Best Entrepreneur of 2021 setting an inspiration for the future generations.He also founded one NGO named 'Love All Serve All' which aims to serve mankind around the world.

Happy Birthday Akash

Happy Birthday Akash you are a very talented person and you are a very good writer my brother.

Each word used in your poems are very meaningful and deep which portrays that you are a great poet and I hope you may enhance your skills like this only

And may you achieve more in your life.

Wishing you a very happy birthday my dearest brother many many happy returns of the day may God bless you and always exhale like this.

With loads of love,

Durlav Bhaiya

13. Trishna Chakraborty

Trishna Chakraborty is a writer from the Hill Station Haflong,Assam. She is the Founder of IYW Publication She is the International Ambassador Of Peace,She is a RJ, and manages many communities under her Publication .She is the English and Hindi Judge of Subash Chandra Bose Community. She is the core member of InkZoid Publication and Word of Souls

Publication.Her writes ups featured in many insta pages and newspapers.She has published her poems and stories on many books,She got the Forever Star Book of Record. She is a cheerful and foodie girl,spreads love everywhere and she is popular in her social circle. You can read her writing and follow her on : Instagram page @herthoughts0616 and @trish.na16

Pyara sa mera akshu

Yad,wohdin mujhe ab bhi he,

Tujh sangh mili jese panktiyan kavita ki he,

Rango me mel anek he,

Par akash se hi toh mera akshu he,

Gulab ka ek who ful he,

Jo mujhe mera sa lagta he,

Jiski chav se sukoon ki rehmat he,

Dil ki chanchalta ki chanak he,

Bhai ek bas mera he,

Qki har behen me uski me hi hun,

Dosti ka nata,dildari yaari hamari,

Char kadmo ki nahi, milo dur ghar, milo kadmo ka sath hamara,

Khushiya bani rahe sada uski,

Hasta khelta rahe who hamesha,

Har koi jane mujhe uske diye nam se,

Khush hoti hun mein,uske zikar se,

Sikhti bhi hun usse, uski hi bate,

Who aage badhta rahe yehi chahat he,

Khilana he use dher sara khana,

Ghumna he har ek Gagan uske sang,

Nili si duniya me hara sa rang,

Pyara babu mere sang.

Trishna Chakraborty

14. Dr Nikita Dudagi

It's Dr. Nikita Dudagi, from Karnataka,a doctor by
profession and a writer by passion.
She's the founder of Words of Soul writing Community
and WOS Publications.She's a part of 200+
anthologies and a Compiler even. A recognised author
by many international writing communities.
She's the Indian Noble Award Holder 2021 for being
the best writer and World Record Holder of Noel
Poetry.She's the Author of the Month March 2021 of
IYW international writing Community.She can write

simultaneously in three different languages,, Kannada, Hindi and English.

Shes believes that no other feeling is greater than being a writer and no one can be a better best friend than a paper and Pen.

आकाश

हर किसीको जोड़कर रखे, रखवाला है जो,

एक जुट बांध लेता है सबको एक डोरी में वो,

निर्मल प्रेम भाव से निभाई हर रिश्ते को जो,

आकाश नामक एक प्यारा सा लड़का है वो

भाई बहन की रिश्ते में आसानी से ढल जाता है वो,

दोस्ती के नाम का पवित्र दीपक है वो,

हुनर से जो सीचता है हर पल खुदको,

जान बसती है लिखावट में जिसकी,

प्यार मुहब्बत से दूरियां तैय किया है,

जिंदगी में आगे बड़ने की ठान ली है,

उतार चढ़ाव से वाकिफ है वो सफर में,

साथ देता है वो ढाल बन हर मुस्कील में।।